Aggression and Bullying
in Adolescence

The PACTS Young Children (1–12) Series: Parent, Adolescent and Child Training Skills

Series Editor: Martin Herbert

The PACTS Adolescence (13–20) Series: Parent, Adolescent and Child Training Skills

Series Editor: Martin Herbert

These editions are published by arrangement with Blackwell Publishing Ltd., Oxford, UK

Aggression and Bullying
in Adolescence

by
Suzanne Guerin and Eilis Hennessy

Series Editor
Martin Herbert

ACER Press

This edition published 2004
by ACER Press
Australian Council for Educational Research Ltd
19 Prospect Hill Road, Camberwell, Victoria, 3124
This edition is published by arrangement with Blackwell Publishers Ltd., Oxford, UK

First published 2002 by the British Psychological Society and Blackwell Publishers Ltd.,
a Blackwell Publishing company
108 Cowley Road, Oxford OX4 1FJ, UK

This edition reprinted from Suzanne Guerin and Eilis Hennessy *Aggression and Bullying* No. 16
in the UK PACTS Series. Edited by Martin Herbert.

Printed by Impact Printing Pty Ltd

National Library of Australia Cataloguing-in-Publication data:

Guerin, Suzanne.
Aggression and bullying in adolescence.
  Bibliography.
  ISBN 0 86431 704 2.
  1. Aggressiveness in adolescence. 2. Bullying.
  I. Hennessy, Eilis. II. Title. (Series : Parent, adolescent
  and child training skills 2; no. 16).

155.518232

Visit our website: www.acerpress.com.au

Contents

Aggression and bullying in adolescence

Introduction

Bullying drove star to steal

BBC News, 18 December 2000

Bullied girl is taken home as protection fails

Electronic Telegraph, 19 February 2000

I was bullied continually from 10 to 15

Electronic Telegraph, 10 September 1999

Torment drove school girl to attempted suicide

Belfast Telegraph, 13 December 1997

In recent years there has been widespread concern among parents, teachers and other people working with children about issues relating to aggression in childhood. This has included concern about the role of violence in the media and its influence on children's behaviour, children displaying aggressive behaviour towards their parents, teachers and peers and the level of bullying that occurs in schools. This concern is reflected in the media headlines cited above. While headlines such as these may heighten concern about aggression and bullying there is also good reason to be optimistic because research has now provided substantial information about the antecedents of aggressive behaviour and the best ways that children and their families can be helped. This book aims to introduce the reader to the topics of aggression and bullying and summarize the findings of research that may be of interest and use to practitioners, students and parents and anyone who works with children.

Aims

This guide aims:

➤ to provide information about aggression and its development during childhood and adolescence;

➤ to introduce bullying behaviour as a subset of aggressive behaviour and to highlight research on the nature and extent of bullying in schools;

➤ to outline some of the characteristics of children involved in bullying and to suggest some signs of bullying that parents and practitioners should be aware of; and

➤ to describe some of the interventions and resources available to practitioners who work with young people.

Objectives

After reading this book you should have:

➤ an understanding of the distinction between typical and atypical aggressive behaviour in childhood;

➤ an awareness of the issues involved in defining bullying behaviour (and some practical suggestions of how to discuss the nature of bullying with groups of children);

➤ an understanding of some of the more common (personal, familial and school) factors associated with children's involvement in bullying and aggressive behaviour;

➤ the knowledge to decide on an appropriate way of measuring the prevalence of bullying behaviour in a school/youth club or other setting;

➤ the knowledge to access appropriate information on bullying that would be useful to parents, teachers and pupils; and

➤ the knowledge to plan, initiate and evaluate a bullying education programme.

Part I: Aggression

What is aggression?

Aggression is not a single type of action. Instead the word refers to a variety of things that people do that cause physical, psychological and/or emotional harm to one another. A child hitting, kicking or punching another child is probably close to most people's stereotype of aggression during childhood but many other types of behaviour would also be classified as aggressive. These can include spreading nasty rumours about someone, deliberately excluding someone from a group, name calling and teasing. Most children come across these forms of aggression at some stage during their school career. Understanding aggression, however, means that it is important to distinguish not just between the different behaviours that are regarded as aggressive but also the differing aims and antecedents of the behaviour.

In an attempt to understand aggression, one distinction frequently made by researchers is between hostile and instrumental aggression. Instrumental (proactive) aggression is behaviour that is intended to obtain something, e.g. pushing a child off a tricycle so that you can have a go yourself. Hostile (reactive) aggression aims specifically to inflict harm or hurt on another person. Understanding this distinction is important because it is the key to understanding one of the early changes in the types of aggressive behaviour that children display. The types of aggression that are typically aimed at causing psychological rather than physical harm are referred to as relational aggression and can include exclusion and gossip.

There is now a considerable body of research on all these types of aggression that can provide an insight into the way in which aggressive behaviours change as children get older, and the personal, family and neighbourhood factors that are associated with differing levels of aggression. Most importantly, this research also provides insights into the ways in which children who are behaving aggressively can be helped. The first part of this booklet will focus on the research findings about aggression in general and the second half focuses on bullying, which is a specific type of aggressive behaviour.

Summary

➤ Definitions of aggressive behaviour include a wide range of negative behaviours, including physical harm (such as hitting or kicking), as well as verbal behaviours and exclusion.

➤ A distinction is made between instrumental aggression (where the intention is to gain something), and hostile aggression (where there is no aim other than to hurt or harm).

The changing nature of aggression

All children and adults show some level of aggressive behaviour and it first becomes visible at an early age. Although we can't tell whether young infants experience feelings of anger in the same way as older children and adults, research has shown that the type of facial expressions usually associated with anger may be seen in infants as young as four months old. Although even younger infants do look displeased if something unpleasant happens to them (e.g. if you take a bottle from an infant's mouth) their expressions are not reliably classified as angry by observers. By the time they are seven months old it is clear that children are using anger to communicate and they will turn their face towards their mother even if she is not the cause of their anger. Thus children seem to be trying to use the facial expression to communicate their feelings to someone else.

By the time they are one year old most infants are capable of some form of retaliatory action and, by the time they are two years old, many have temper tantrums, as conflict over autonomy becomes more central to their lives. By this age, children are also interested in their own possessions and will attempt to keep them away from a peer who shows an interest. At this age, conflict is quite common during peer interaction and can be sparked by many factors such as two children wishing to play with the same toy. This aggression is typically 'instrumental' because its primary aim is to acquire or retain possession of the object rather than to hurt the other person.

By the time children start school, physical aggression is typically much less common than it was during the preschool years, although verbal aggression (including shouting and name-calling) typically increases. One reason for the decrease in physical aggression is the improvement in language skills that allows children not only to communicate their own needs more effectively but also to use verbal negotiation instead of physical aggression when dealing with a situation that has potential for conflict.

During the early school years we begin to see less instrumental aggression and more hostile aggression, i.e. aggression aimed primarily at hurting the other person rather than simply taking his/her possessions. One reason that has been suggested for this change is that older children are better able to infer the intention and motives of others so they can distinguish between potentially threatening and benign situations. When children believe that another person is trying to hurt them, they are more likely to act with an aggressive response towards that person.

There are also a number of important changes that take place in aggressive behaviour in the transition from childhood to adolescence. One very noticeable and worrying change is the fact that aggression is more likely to result in injury or, in extreme cases, death. Loeber and Hay (1997) argue that this is partly due to the increase in physical strength associated with adolescence and puberty but also to an increase in the use of weapons in conflict situations. The second change that they identify is a move towards collective forms of violence in which groups of youths may join together in situations of conflict. A third change associated with aggression during adolescence is that a small number will eventually strike out at a familiar authority figure such as a schoolteacher or parent and rates of parent–child conflict generally increase. Fourthly, adolescence is marked by an increase in cross-gender conflict. Such cross-gender conflict is much less common during childhood when children tend to associate primarily with their own sex.

Summary

➢ All children can be expected to display some aggressive behaviour. During the preschool years this aggression is usually focused on getting or keeping something they want.
➢ As children get older, their use of physical aggression typically decreases but it is sometimes replaced by verbal aggression such as name-calling or teasing.
➢ For the majority of children this aggressive behaviour should not be seen as problematic and will disappear as they learn to communicate better with people and as they learn to judge other people's intentions.

Are boys more aggressive than girls?

One answer to this question might be: it depends on what you mean by aggression. If you define aggression as physical or verbal attack on another person, then there are a number of research studies that suggest that boys are more aggressive than girls. However, if you include relational aggression in this definition (behaviour such as excluding individuals from the group and saying nasty things about them) then the difference between boys and girls looks much less striking. Unfortunately, most research on aggression has focused almost exclusively on physical and verbal aggression so we know much less about the way in which relational aggression emerges during childhood. Dunn's (1993) work also suggests that there may be fewer sex differences in aggressive behaviour when sibling groups are studied. Her work revealed that boys and girls showed fairly high levels of physical aggression with their siblings.

The gender differences that have been described in childhood typically first emerge in the preschool years. During infancy few researchers report any gender differences in aggression, though this typically changes around three years of age. In particular, in naturalistic settings (e.g. in children's homes and preschools) boys have been observed to engage in more verbal and physical conflict and to be more forceful in their use of aggression. There are a number of possible reasons for these differences. Firstly, a number of studies have suggested that boys are more impulsive than girls and that this may lead them into many more conflicts over the possession of objects. A typical example of this would be the impulsive grabbing of an interesting toy from another child; this upsets or threatens the other child and some form of conflict results. In this way, impulsivity may bring boys into more situations where there is potential for conflict. Secondly, gender differences in aggression may be further influenced by girls' greater abilities to use verbal negotiating skills to prevent conflict escalating into aggression. The differences may, in part, be influenced by biological differences between boys and girls and by differing social expectations for the display of aggression.

These different social expectations have been well illustrated by research findings that show that adults interpret ambiguous and potentially angry and aggressive responses differently depending on whether they believe they are looking at a girl or a boy. For example, adults may label a reaction 'aggressive' when they believe that they have been watching a girl's behaviour and 'assertive' when they believe that they have been watching a boy. Research also suggests that there are gender differences in the ways in which boys are treated by their parents, particularly fathers. Fathers typically engage in more boisterous and physically energetic play with their sons than with their daughters so boys are more socialized into this kind of activity. Research findings like these suggest that, in our society, we are more tolerant of low levels of aggressive behaviour in boys than in girls. This difference has potentially significant implications for children's development because the consequence may be that boys are less likely to experience (and therefore expect) negative consequences of aggressive acts than girls.

Summary

➢ Boys tend to show more overt physical and verbal aggression than girls. However, this gender difference does not seem to apply to siblings' interactions and does not take relational aggression into account.
➢ In our society we may be more tolerant of physical and verbal aggression in boys, which may influence the development of their attitudes to aggression.

When is aggressive behaviour a problem?

For the majority of children aggressive behaviour will not become a problem, even though they may occasionally behave aggressively. There is also a small minority of children whose aggressive behaviour is clearly problematic and may include, for example, high levels of fighting with peers, cruelty to people or animals, and/or attacks on people. Such a child's parents or teachers would have no difficulty in deciding that he/she needs some form of therapeutic intervention. There is, however, another small group of children whose aggressive behaviour falls somewhere between the typical levels of aggression shown by most children and the extreme level of aggressive behaviour just described. Deciding whether children in this group are in need of therapeutic intervention may be a more difficult decision for parents and practitioners.

One useful guideline for parents is that aggressive behaviour is a cause for greater concern when accompanied by other antisocial behaviours such as failure to comply with parents and/or teachers, defiance of authority figures, lying or stealing. Aggression is also considered problematic when it has been going on for a considerable period of time – thus excluding occasional acts of aggression or short periods of heightened aggressive behaviour. For example, temper tantrums are relatively common among under five-year-olds, but if they persist at the same frequency and intensity beyond the age of five, they would be a cause for concern.

One answer to the question 'When is aggressive behaviour a problem?' is: when the child also displays other antisocial behaviours and when he/she has been behaving aggressively for a number of months or years. Of course parents, teachers or others working with children may also wish to seek therapeutic intervention for children when aggressive behaviour begins to interfere with their everyday activities even if their behaviour does not seem to fit in with these other criteria: for example, if one child's aggressive behaviour towards a sibling is causing problems for the family, or if aggression is resulting in a child being excluded from their peer group in school.

Summary

➤ When deciding whether a child's aggressive behaviours are a problem or not important factors include the length of time the behaviours have been occurring, as well as the impact of the behaviours on others.

Factors related to aggression

We know that the vast majority of children display a certain amount of aggression, whether verbal or physical, and in this section we will consider why this should be the case. On the whole, research on this topic has focused on the factors that are related to physically aggressive behaviour, such as poverty, the availability of aggressive responses and beliefs about the effectiveness of aggression.

Environment

Children grow up in complex environments extending from the immediate family and school to the neighbourhood, city/region, religious group, culture and country. All these environments exert an influence on the developing child and would be too numerous to discuss in detail in this section. We are, therefore, focusing on two environmental influences that research has demonstrated have a major influence on many children's development. The first of these is neighbourhood poverty and the second is television violence.

Neighbourhood poverty

In their comprehensive review of aggression and antisocial behaviour in childhood and adolescence, Coie and Dodge (1998) point to a substantial body of research which has linked physical aggression and poverty in the USA. In particular, studies of the rates of violent crime show that it is not distributed evenly across geographic regions but rather is concentrated in crowded urban areas that are typically associated with poverty. This does not mean that poverty is always associated with violence; rather poverty is one of a number of risk factors that may increase the chances of aggressive behaviour in some cultural contexts. On its own, poverty may be of no significance but if it is combined with other risks it may result in higher levels of aggression.

In addition to pointing to the association between urban poverty in the USA and violence, researchers have addressed the question of why poverty should be a risk factor at all. One suggestion is that, when children are young, the effects of poverty are not directly on the children but rather on parents. All parents experience a certain amount of stress in their role as caregivers and poverty may increase these stresses. Family poverty may influence parents' disciplinary practices, their ability to successfully supervise their children's activities and the nature of the attachment relationship between parents and children. In this way, the children may experience the effects of poverty through its impact on their parents' behaviour.

As children get older, living in an area with high rates of crime and the presence of neighbourhood gangs and drug abuse may have a direct impact on them. Older children may be more likely to witness violent crime or to know someone who has experienced the effects of violence. It may increase children's chances of meeting peer groups who engage in antisocial activities and becoming involved with those activities. However, it is clear that poverty is only one of a number of factors that influence the development of children living in these areas and that the majority of children will not themselves engage in violent activities simply because their family is poor. Some research findings suggest that parents, in these circumstances, who remain extremely vigilant of their children's activities well into their teenage years, may reduce the risk of their involvement in antisocial activities.

Television violence

Concern about television violence and its effects on children has been a feature of the debates about the role of media in children's lives for many years. In the 1960s, children who took part in psychological research on the effects of viewing aggression saw an adult behaving aggressively on television and since then this research has been widely cited in the debate on television violence. There have been a number of experimental laboratory studies that demonstrate that televised aggression can have an immediate impact on the child's behaviour. There are also longitudinal studies that have kept track of children's television watching habits and explored the relationship between the amount of aggressive television watched and the extent of aggressive activities displayed. On the basis of a number of such studies in different countries, Coie and Dodge (1998) conclude that with few exceptions, the level of viewing of televised violence predicts aggression three years later. Their conclusion holds even when the level of aggression of the children is controlled statistically. In other words, if a child who is very aggressive and a child who has low levels of aggression watch substantial amounts of aggression on television, both will show increases in their levels of aggression. It seems that the link between television watching and violence is not simply due to the fact that children who are inclined to behave more aggressively are also attracted to aggressive television programmes.

Why does television have an effect on aggression? Children learn new forms of behaviour by watching aggression on television and they may at the same time learn that it is okay for some people (e.g. 'good guys') to behave aggressively. In other words, they may learn a new way of being aggressive and at the same time find a justification for that behaviour (because the victim 'deserved it'). Just as an angry adult may believe that he/she is justified in 'beeping' angrily at another motorist 'because of their bad driving', so children may learn to justify their own aggressive acts. It is also possible that watching television heroes who don't experience any negative consequences of aggressive behaviour may reduce children's expectations of negative consequences of their own aggressive behaviour.

Television is not the only place where children may view aggressive behaviour, of course, and it is very important to consider the other ways in which new aggressive responses may become available to children, and the other contexts in which they may develop beliefs about the likely consequences of aggression. These issues are considered below.

Learning aggressive responses

Imagine a parent driving home from work with two young children in the back of the car. The traffic is bad and the parent's anger increases with each perceived fault in other drivers: they don't move quickly enough when the lights turn green, they fail to make best use of gaps in oncoming traffic to turn right and so on. The parent shouts or calls names and beeps the car horn aggressively. When the family is at home, the very same parent is horrified to find the children name-calling and behaving aggressively to one another in disputes over toys. Is the children's behaviour linked to the parent's? We know that children learn aggressive responses when they observe them in adults and older children. These aggressive 'models' seem to influence children's behaviour in a number of ways. Firstly, they can teach the child a new form of aggressive behaviour – in this case name-calling. Secondly, they can influence children to believe that it is acceptable to behave in that way, that nothing bad will happen as a consequence. Thirdly, this behaviour can produce emotional arousal in the onlookers; thus the children can themselves begin to feel angry because of the behaviour they are observing in the parent.

Of course parents are not the only possible source of 'models' for children. Children also learn from the reactions of their teachers, older children, their sporting heroes and their television heroes. If these models 'teach' children that aggression is acceptable, then they will increase the chances that the children will themselves behave aggressively.

Beliefs about aggression

Unfortunately there are many circumstances in which children learn, through their own experiences or through observing others, that aggression can produce a desirable outcome. If a child pushes another child off a bicycle in order to get a ride on the bicycle themselves and that behaviour is not checked, then the child has got first-hand experience of the value of using aggression. Coie and Dodge (1998) suggest that environments that allow children to be exposed to aggression, to try out aggressive behaviour, or to see aggression being rewarded are likely to increase the chances that the children will behave aggressively. Indeed, one feature of the gender difference in aggression between boys and girls is that boys typically anticipate fewer negative and more positive consequences of aggression than girls.

Summary

➢ The development of aggressive behaviour can be influenced by environmental factors such as the presence of examples of aggressive behaviour at home, on the television or in the neighbourhood.
➢ Children who learn that an aggressive reaction is appropriate and acceptable are more likely to display aggression themselves.
➢ Children can develop positive beliefs about aggression, particularly if they identify rewards from aggressive behaviours.

Individual differences in aggression

Not all children growing up in disadvantaged urban areas display high levels of aggressive behaviour, and not all children who observe television violence imitate that violence in their own play with their friends. Some girls show high levels of verbal and physical aggression, while some boys show very low levels of verbal and physical aggression. Thus, the general conditions described in the last section that increase children's likelihood of behaving aggressively do not have the same impact on all children. To fully understand aggressive behaviour, therefore, we must focus not only on the factors that typically increase aggression but also on the factors that influence an individual child's level of aggression. Indeed it is these individual differences that are usually of greatest concern to parents and teachers and other people working with children. There is now a substantial volume of research devoted to understanding individual differences in aggressive behaviour, and this can provide us with a rich source of information on the factors that could have an impact on a child's behaviour.

Is a four-year-old who behaves aggressively in preschool also likely to be-have aggressively when he/she is eight or eighteen or thirty-eight? This ques-tion of the extent to which aggressive behaviour is a persistent feature of an individual's responses over long periods of time has now been addressed in a number of longitudinal studies that have followed groups of children over many years (in some cases into adulthood). On the whole, the findings from these studies suggest that aggressive behaviour does seem to be consistent over time. For example, Olweus (1979) has demonstrated that the amount of physical and verbal aggression expressed at ages six to ten years is related to the level of aggression directed towards peers four years later. The most im-pressive evidence, however, comes from a 22-year longitudinal study of 600 individuals originally seen at age eight (Huesmann *et al.*, 1984). At that time, the children were asked to name classmates who behaved in certain ways including aggressively (e.g. 'who pushes or shoves children?'). Aggression was measured several times in the following years. Children who were rated as aggressive by their peers when they were eight years old tended to be rated as aggressive by their peers years later. Those who were rated as aggressive by their peers tended to rate themselves as more aggressive, to rate others as aggressive and to see the world as an aggressive place. Those who were rated as highly aggressive at age eight were three times more likely to have a police record by the time they were adults. At age 30, significantly more of them had been convicted of criminal behaviour, were aggressive towards their spouses, and tended to punish their own children severely. This level of consistency from age 8 to age 30 should alert us to the need to intervene at an early age when children appear to be displaying a level of aggressive behaviour above that of their peer group. Research that has identified factors related to indi-vidual levels of aggression has helped researchers to focus on possible ways of helping children to reduce their aggressive behaviour. In the sections that follow, some of the main factors are considered in turn.

Family influences

When discussing research that links poverty with increased risk of aggres-sion, it was mentioned that the main impact of poverty on young children might be through the kind of stresses that it causes for parents. Much of the research on individual differences in aggression has looked within families and at the way in which family members relate to one another. Such research suggests that parent–child relationships, parental warmth and disciplinary practices may be particularly important in terms of predicting children's aggressive behaviour.

Parent–child relationships

Towards the end of the first year of life all infants begin to show a strong pref-erence for the people who typically look after them, including parents, older siblings, caregivers, grandparents, uncles and aunts. The British psychiatrist John Bowlby believed that this display of preference for these people was an expression of an underlying attachment relationship between the infant and the adult. Bowlby went on to argue that attachment relationships are impor-tant for children's feelings of security but also for their longer-term ability to trust other people and have positive relationships with them. Except in very exceptional circumstances, children will form attachment relationships with one or more adults; however, not all these relationships are equivalent in terms of the infant's subjective sense of security. Thus some children have secure attachment relationships. Within such relationships the child is read-ily comforted when upset, feels free to explore the environment and devel-ops a sense of trust in other people. However, some children have insecure attachment relationships and these children are not readily comforted by the presence of their caregivers – they may appear unwilling to explore their surroundings and some research suggests that may display specific negative behaviours towards other people.

Research findings do not consistently point to direct links between insecure attachment and aggressive behaviour. Thus, insecure attachment on its own may not predict aggression but when it is associated with another risk factor, such as poverty, it may result in higher levels of aggression.

Parental warmth

The nature of the attachment between parent and child tells us something about their relationship. The level of warmth between them is another way of measuring this relationship. Some research suggests that the absence of maternal affection is associated with increased levels of problem behaviour. Specifically, Bates and Bayles (1988) found that mothers who displayed high levels of affection for their children had children with lower levels of problem behaviour.

Disciplinary practices

Parents of aggressive children have been found to employ more power-assertive methods of discipline, using physical punishment rather than verbal explanation or reasoning as their way of dealing with misbehaviour. To social learning theorists this finding suggests that two processes may be at work in these situations. First, the parents may be modelling aggressive behaviour to their children, who go on to imitate what they see. Second, these parents may be interacting with their children in ways that actually promote aggression.

Research has also found that it is common for families of aggressive children to display a troublesome pattern of interactions that has been termed 'coercive family process'. These households are characterized by very few friendly cooperative comments or behaviours and by a high rate of hostile and negative responses. Commonly, the parents spend a good deal of time scolding, telling off and threatening the children while the children whine, complain or disobey the parents and also tease and frustrate one another. In such environments, aggression is used as a means of stopping or escaping from these sorts of aversive stimuli. For example a girl may tease and taunt her older brother who hits her to make her stop; this, in turn, leads the mother to hit the brother for hitting his sister. This pattern is described as coercion because the family members achieve their goals through threats, commands and other coercive behaviours rather than through cooperative, prosocial means. Children who have learned this style of interaction at home also display aggression in other settings and often go on to delinquency and other serious forms of antisocial behaviour. In contrast to these coercive patterns of family interaction, other families show patterns of reinforcing positive behaviour (commenting on work well done, talking about disagreements rather than resorting to conflict) that are associated with non-aggressive behaviour in children.

The British Government's decision in May 2001 to allow childminders to smack children they are minding, when they have parental permission, has reopened a long debate about the effects of physical punishment on children's behaviour. Physical punishment is just one type of power-assertive technique that may be used by some parents to get their children to behave as they wish. Others include direct commands without explanation ('You do it because I told you to'), threats ('If you don't do it Father Christmas won't bring you a present') and deprivation (sent to bed without supper). British research suggests that harsh discipline at ages eight and nine was associated with delinquency in boys (Farrington & Hawkins, 1991).

Mental processes

Children, like adults, differ from one another in their interpretation of the world around them. Research suggests that the extent to which we interpret other people's behaviour as hostile will determine the extent to which we are inclined to behave aggressively towards them. Children who typically display high levels of aggression show certain cognitive differences from their classmates. For example, their level of moral reasoning tends to be lower and they are less likely to take into account someone's motives when making a moral judgement about a story character. In addition these children typically show less empathy with peers who are distressed.

In a series of experiments, Dodge and his colleagues (Dodge, 1985) found that children differ in their attributions of other people's intentions and that these differences in attributions are meaningfully related to displays of aggression. Their studies typically involved videotaped episodes in which one child is harmed or provoked by a peer whose intentions are unclear. In these situations aggressive children are much more likely to attribute hostile or malicious motives to the provoker. When cues are provided to suggest that the provoker's intentions were not hostile, aggressive children have more difficulty in understanding and using these cues. Further research suggests that children who are aggressive focus more on aggressive social cues, and evaluate aggressive responses as less morally 'bad' and more acceptable. These findings suggest that children who behave aggressively differ from other children not only in their behaviour but also in their interpretation of the world; in other words, they see it is a more threatening place, and aggressive behaviour as more acceptable within it.

Peers and aggressive behaviour

Having friends and getting on with other children is an important aspect of any child's life. Not only can you have a lot of fun with your friends but there are also important things that you can learn when you are with them. For example, mixing with other children and making friendships gives each child a chance to learn about the thoughts and feelings of other people. Groups of friends also provide an opportunity for beginning to display qualities such as leadership, which are not usually displayed in adult company. One major concern, therefore, about children who display high levels of aggression is that they are frequently rejected by their peer group. This means that they miss out on the very learning opportunities that might give them a chance to learn many of the social skills that they need.

Research suggests that aggressive children are likely to be rejected by their peers. Further research suggests that children who display angry outbursts and those who display instrumental aggression are among those most likely to be rejected. Aggressive behaviour is also more likely to be associated with rejection for girls than for boys, possibly because levels of aggression are typically higher among groups of boys. Longitudinal research, which has followed children's development over a number of years, suggests that peer rejection further compounds the problems of children who display aggressive behaviour, over and above the kinds of problems expected from their aggression. For example, Patterson and Bank (1989) found that 10-year-olds who were rejected by their peer group were more likely to be involved in antisocial activity two years later. Another study by Coie *et al.* (1995) found that boys who were both rejected and aggressive at age nine tended to become increasingly aggressive over the following years, whereas aggression tended to decrease among other boys in the study.

The impact of personal levels of aggression on a child's ability to fit in with their peer group is only one of the issues relevant to peers and aggressive behaviour. Another long-standing cause of concern is the likely effect on a child of having friends who are aggressive. Although there are a number of studies which suggest that adolescents are at risk of increased levels of antisocial behaviour if they associate with peers who engage in antisocial activities, these are not studies of aggression *per se*. While the measures of antisocial behaviour may have included questions on aggression we don't know if these are as likely to be influenced by peers as other behaviours.

Summary

➤ Within the family, parent–child relations and disciplinary practices have been linked to aggression. Where relationships among family members are warm and parents do not use power-assertive disciplinary practices, children are least likely to behave aggressively.
➤ Children's ability to reason about what is morally right or wrong and their ability to interpret social situations may also be linked to their level of aggressive behaviour. As children grow, their peer group becomes more important, and friends can encourage or reject aggressive behaviour.

Tackling aggressive behaviour

The previous section identified a number of factors that have been linked to aggressive behaviour, including family factors and mental processes. Researchers have been able to identify how intervening in these areas can help reduce aggressive behaviour in children. This section outlines two of a number of methods that have been developed to help tackle aggressive behaviour, parent management training and problem-solving skills training.

Parent management training

Understanding family relationships can be an important part of understanding aggressive behaviour and can also provide a focus for intervention to reduce aggression. Parent management training refers to therapeutic interventions that aim to alter the nature of the interactions between children and their parents in order to decrease children's aggressive behaviour. The assumption underlying these interventions is that parents may be inadvertently providing an environment in which their child's aggression is maintained. One of the great advantages of this type of intervention is that training allows parents to apply the necessary intervention in the very environment where the problem of aggression is found. In addition, parents spend far more time with their children than therapists or teachers so they are in an ideal position to ensure that the intervention is applied consistently and for an extended period of time.

Initially parent management training involves teaching parents to identify, define and observe their child's aggressive behaviour. These must be the first skills learned if parents are to carry out the reinforcement and punishment that are part of the next stage of the intervention. Reinforcement of desirable behaviour and punishment of negative behaviour are based on the principles of learning theory, which states that behaviour which is rewarded is more likely to be repeated and behaviour which is punished is less likely to be repeated. During this phase of the training a range of suitable rewards and punishments are suggested to parents so that they can choose ones that are most appropriate to their child's age and temperament. Rewards could be verbal and include praise or positive comments about the child's behaviour or they might include tokens such as stars on a chart or a points system. It is most important that parents are taught to use only mild punishments to avoid the punishment becoming part of the problem. Suitable mild punishments can include the withdrawal of privileges such as pocket money, television watching or trips to the local shops. The next phase of training gives parents the opportunity to practise using these techniques in role-play situations. Parents are encouraged to keep careful records of their child's aggressive behaviour so that they can tell whether their new skills are having the desired effect. Changes in behaviour are monitored by the therapist, who can advise parents on changes to reward schedules should these be needed.

Research on parent management training programmes suggests that they produce significant reductions in problem behaviour and that these reductions persist over many years. A review of such studies may be found in Kazdin (1987).

Problem-solving skills training

Because children who show high levels of aggressive behaviour seem to interpret other people's behaviour as aggressive, addressing this perception of the world can be a useful basis for therapeutic intervention. Problem-solving skills training focuses on the way in which children interpret other people's activities and motivations and aims to give them the necessary skills to solve social problems without resorting to aggression. Thus, this approach focuses on the way in which children think about social problems rather than on the way in which they behave. The therapy is based on cognitive development theory, which holds that our behaviour is rooted in our interpretation of the world. According to this theory, altering a child's interpretation of the world should in turn alter their behaviour.

Problem-solving skills training typically involves individual children or small groups working with a therapist who presents them with pictures or stories about other children. The pictures and stories are designed to elicit children's views of other people's motives and the likely consequences of their behaviour. When children initially interpret characters' motives as aggressive (in situations that are ambiguous) they are encouraged, through discussion with the therapist or the rest of the group, to come up with alternative motives. Thus, over time children are introduced to the possibility that there are many possible motives for people's actions and they are encouraged to begin to use these other interpretations in real life situations. The stories and pictures can also be used to encourage children to think about the consequences of aggression for those involved. The therapist can use discussion to explore what children believe are the likely consequences of hurting someone else, both for the aggressor and the victim.

Helping children to generalize from pictures and stories to the real world can be facilitated by getting children to talk about their own experiences and how they decided on the course of action that would be best. Here the therapist can also offer accounts of their experiences in order to provide models of non-aggressive ways to solve problems. Many therapists will encourage parents and teachers to become involved in the training process through the use of rewards for appropriate behaviour in social settings. This can help to reinforce children's growing interpersonal skills.

Evaluation of a number of different problem-solving skills training programmes suggests that they can result in significant reductions in problem behaviour. However, Kazdin (1993) argues that they are more effective with older rather than younger children.

Having discussed the research relating to aggression in general, the next section of this booklet considers bullying as a specific form of aggression. It reviews some of the research in this area and offers a range of suggestions to those working with children who may be concerned about levels of bullying.

Summary

➢ Having identified some of the factors that appear to be associated with aggressive behaviour, researchers have been able to develop interventions.

> ➤ Parent management training involves helping parents to alter the nature of their interactions with their children in order to decrease their child's aggressive behaviour.
> ➤ Problem-solving skills training provides children with the necessary skills to solve social problems without resorting to aggression.

Hints for parents

Resolving conflicts

Sharing can be difficult for children of all ages so don't be surprised if there are conflicts when friends call around. Although sharing should be encouraged, it may be helpful if you allow your child to put one or two prized toys away when a friend is coming if these are likely to be a source of conflict. Remember to praise your child whenever he/she shares and/or takes turns with a friend.

Verbal negotiation

Encourage your child to use verbal negotiation whenever possible by modelling these skills through your own actions. Talk to your child about the many ways in which conflict can be solved without resorting to aggression. Encourage your child to think about the consequences of aggression – how people can get badly hurt or how someone will feel if excluded from activities.

Methods for encouraging positive behaviour and discouraging negative behaviour

What should you do if your child or a child whom you teach seems to be displaying problematic aggressive behaviour?

> ➤ Decide on the desirable behaviour that you wish to encourage, e.g. requesting a toy instead of taking it from another child/sibling. Whenever the child displays this behaviour this should be rewarded with a positive comment, e.g. 'Well done, you asked for that very politely'.
> ➤ When the inappropriate behaviour occurs (e.g. grabbing the toy/hitting another child) then there should be a clear negative consequence, e.g. withdrawal of some privilege such as TV watching or going to the shops.
> ➤ Be consistent in your responses to the child's behaviour – always reward the desired behaviour and apply the consequences for the undesired behaviour.

definitions of bullying that correspond more closely to adults' views. We know that, for instance, older children are more likely to report forms of indirect bullying (exclusion etc) than younger children, suggesting that their definition has broadened to include behaviour that is not physical. Secondly, for the practitioner dealing with children who have been distressed by something that has happened within their peer group, it will always be important to understand the child's perspective about the events as well as to consider whether it fits with research definitions of a bully/victim situation.

For the purposes of this booklet we have included both types of research, i.e. research that uses the 'classical' definitions of bullying as well as research that has focused more on children's views.

Summary

➢ Definitions of bullying include a wide range of verbal and physical behaviours, as well as forms of exclusion and intimidation.
➢ In distinguishing bullying from aggression, researchers have stressed the social nature of bullying, as well as its recurrence over time.
➢ It is important to explore children's definition of bullying as it has been shown that they do not always reflect research definitions.

Where does bullying take place?

Bullying can occur in any place where young people interact. This includes school, at home, at clubs or in the wider community. However, much of the research work has focused on bullying in schools, mainly because of the amount of time that young people spend in school. Also, from the point of view of research, it has been relatively easy to access school children and examine their understanding of, and involvement in, bullying. Finally, it is through the school that the difficulties experienced by those involved in bullying can be brought to the attention of the practitioner. For these reasons this discussion will focus primarily on bullying at school, including prevalence and intervention. However, the information can be applied to other group situations as well.

Summary

➢ While a large majority of the research has focused on bullying in school, it can occur among groups of children in any environment.

Types of bullying

The most common forms of bullying are verbal and physical abuse, such as name-calling and physical attacks. Research in schools in Britain and Ireland found that name-calling was the most common form of bullying, followed by physical bullying. Other behaviours include psychological or relational aggression such as excluding a child from a group, intimidation and threats. Some researchers have suggested that it is helpful to think of name-calling and physical harm as 'direct' bullying. In contrast, exclusion or spreading rumours might be regarded as 'indirect' bullying, similar to the concept of relational aggression discussed earlier. What all these behaviours have in common is that they cause hurt and distress. From these accounts of the many forms of bullying behaviour, it is clear that it can involve all the types of aggressive behaviour mentioned in Part I.

Summary

> Name-calling and physical harm are the most commonly reported forms of bullying.
> Other types of bullying include 'indirect' harm, such as spreading rumours and exclusion.

How common is bullying?

There is now a substantial volume of research evidence from studies conducted in schools in Britain and Ireland on the prevalence of bullying behaviour. Unfortunately, the figures suggest that the problem is very widespread and that most children will experience or witness bullying at some point in their school career.

One of the first large-scale studies in Britain was undertaken by Whitney and Smith (1993) and looked at reported involvement in bullying among 6,700 pupils in primary and secondary schools. Children were asked to provide information anonymously in a questionnaire on whether they had ever been bullied themselves and whether they had ever bullied anyone else. They found that 27 per cent of pupils in primary school and 10 per cent of pupils in secondary school reported that they had been bullied. Within these groups, 10 per cent and 4 per cent respectively had been bullied 'once a week' or more often. The numbers of pupils who reported that they had bullied someone were smaller: 12 per cent of primary school pupils and 6 per cent of those in secondary schools. A small proportion engaged in bullying behaviour on a regular basis, 4 per cent of primary school pupils and 1 per cent of secondary school pupils had bullied 'once a week' or more often. Interestingly, this study found that while there were few gender differences in reports of being bullied, more boys than girls were involved in bullying others.

In Ireland, O'Moore *et al.* (1997) conducted a nationwide study of bullying in primary and secondary schools and reported somewhat higher figures for involvement in bullying. This study found that 31 per cent of primary school pupils and 15 per cent of those in secondary schools had been bullied at some point in the previous term, while 4 per cent and 2 per cent respectively were bullied once a week or more often. In addition, 26 per cent in primary and 15 per cent in secondary school reported that they had bullied others, while 1 per cent of each group had done so once a week or more often. This study found more consistent gender differences than the British study, with more boys in primary and secondary schools reporting being bullied and bullying others.

These figures from Britain and Ireland indicate that bullying is less common in secondary schools than primary schools. Such findings have led researchers to investigate whether there is a general tendency for involvement in bullying to decrease as children grow older. There is some support for this idea. For example, Whitney and Smith (1993) and O'Moore *et al.* (1997) found that the number of victims of bulling tended to decrease with increasing age. However, Whitney and Smith's (1993) figures for children involved in bullying were more constant and only declined slightly. O'Moore *et al.* (1997) found that the reports of pupils in the first year of secondary school had very low reported levels of bullying; however, these figures rose during the second year and did not return to those low levels again.

So it would seem that while the trend among victims' reports is for the incidence to decrease, this is not the case for bullies. One possible explanation for these findings is that, as children grow older, they become better equipped to deal with bullying. However, it is possible that this decline represents a decrease in reported victimization rather than actual involvement. Perhaps older children are less willing to report that they have been bullied than are younger children. It is interesting to note that, while the number of victims decreases, the number of bullies does not.

Despite some reports of declining numbers of victims with increasing age, overall these research findings suggests that bullying is a common feature of the lives of many primary and secondary school children. Fortunately the proportion of children who experience regular bullying is small but this is the group that may be most seriously affected by their experiences, as we will see in the next section.

Summary

➢ Approximately one-third of children in primary school report that they have been bullied in a given term, while around 10 to 15 per cent had bullied others.
➢ Of those involved in bullying, the majority report infrequent involvement, with very few reporting being involved 'once a week' or more often.
➢ There is less reported involvement in bullying in secondary school. There appears to be a decreasing trend in reported involvement in bullying as children get older.

Effects of bullying

If bullying is common in school then does this mean that we should accept it as part of life and maybe even a preparation for life outside school? The answer to this question is definitely 'no'. The experience of being bullied can make a child's school life absolutely miserable, and allowing bullies to continue their aggressive behaviour may be effectively rewarding their actions. Research also suggests that involvement in bullying has long-term negative effects for both victims and bullies. Because of these negative consequences in the short and long term, it is very important that bullying is tackled effectively while children are still in school.

A large number of books and articles have considered the effects of bullying on the victim. Some of the reported effects include reduced self-esteem and difficulty concentrating (Smith and Sharp, 1994, Olweus, 1993). Smith (1991) also reports that the rejection suffered by victims can also predict later difficulties. One study, which looked at the association between involvement in bullying and common health symptoms, found that symptoms such as sleeping difficulties, bedwetting, headaches and tummy aches were all associated with bullying. In some extreme cases, bullying has also been associated with suicide among young people.

Considering the effect of involvement on bullies, work by Olweus has found that bullies were more likely to engage in antisocial behaviour in adulthood, which included involvement in criminal behaviour. In addition, Farrington (1993) suggested that fathers who bullied were more likely to have children who were bullies. Finally, aside from those directly involved in bullying, research has suggested that those who witness bullying also suffer from the experience.

Summary

➤ Bullying has a wide range of short- and long-term negative effects for the victim, including low self-esteem and increased reporting of bedwetting, stomach ache and sleeping difficulties.

➤ Bullying has also been associated with long-term negative effects on the bully, which centre on continuing aggressive behaviour and involvement in criminal activities.

Who is involved in bullying?

Personal characteristics of children involved in bullying

A large body of research has considered the personal characteristics of children involved in bullying. Readers may be familiar with the traditional image of the physically big, confident and popular bully and the small, weak and unpopular victims. However, research suggests that this is not necessarily the case. Researchers have examined factors such as popularity, physical strength, physical defects, self-esteem, confidence and attitudes towards violence among children who bully and children who are victimized. Excellent reviews of this research can be found in Byrne (1993) and Olweus (1993). In this section we summarize some of the main research findings to see if the stereotypes are confirmed.

If we consider first the image of the bully as physically large then the research suggests some support for this view. Research finds that bullies are described as being physically stronger than their victims, with a positive attitude to aggression and violence. Olweus (1993) describes bullies as having an aggressive reaction pattern. We know from the research on aggression that children who are aggressive see the world as a more aggressive place and have lower levels of moral reasoning than other children. Research also provides some support for the view that bullies are confident, with findings suggesting that they are assertive and have a positive view of themselves. Research findings do not, however, confirm the idea that bullies are popular. Perhaps surprisingly, children who bully are more popular than their victims but they are not as popular as children who are not involved in bullying. Research on bullies' school performance suggests that they are typically performing at an average or below average level compared to the rest of the class.

Research on the characteristics of victims suggests that they are physically weaker than bullies, more anxious and insecure, with a negative attitude towards aggression and violence. Olweus (1993) describes victims as having an anxious reaction pattern. Victims are also described as having a negative view of themselves. Even more than bullies, children who are victimized find themselves outside the main group of children with very low levels of popularity. Because victims have frequently been stereotyped as having a different physical appearance from other children (for example, wearing glasses or being overweight) research has concentrated on physical appearance and ability among bullies and victims. Other studies have found that obesity and physical handicaps were most common among victims; however, they were also more common among bullies than other children. Finally, research has found that children who are victimized are typically performing at an average or below average level in school, making their academic level very similar to that of bullies.

Overall this research seems to suggest that there are few physical differences between bullies and their victims with the exception of strength. On a psychological level there are some differences, particularly in relation to confidence and assertiveness. However, it is important to keep in mind that children may be involved in bullying without fitting any of these descriptions.

Not all research has focused exclusively on bullies and victims, and some recent research has provided interesting insights into a variety of different ways in which children can be involved in bullying behaviour. Initially this research focused on the possibility that there might be more than one type of bully and victim. Researchers have distinguished between 'passive' and 'provocative' victims and between 'bullies' and 'anxious bullies'. Passive victims fit the description of victims of bullying described above. In contrast, provocative victims irritate children around them, provoking a negative reaction in others. Anxious bullies, unlike the description above, are much less confident and secure; Olweus (1993) refers to these as 'henchmen' who provide moral support to bullies. Researchers have also identified a group of children called bully/victims, who are involved in bullying other children but are also bullied by others. Very little is known about the characteristics of bully/victims.

More recently, researchers in Scandinavia have expanded the possibility of involvement in bullying well beyond the classification of bullies and victims. Apart from the bully, the victim, and the bully/victim, children can take on the roles of the defender of the victim, the reinforcer of the bully, and the outsider. Taking the wide range of levels of involvement outlined here, it is highly likely that most, if not all, children are 'involved' in bullying in some way at some time in the school career.

Family factors associated with bullying

While research has identified some typical characteristics of bullies and victims, it is unclear whether these characteristics are the cause or the consequence of the type of involvement. In order to understand involvement in bullying, researchers have looked to the family to see if those involved in bullying showed any particular familial characteristics. In the earlier sections on aggression, the influence of factors such as child rearing practices (particularly around discipline) suggest that aggressive behaviours may be modelled in the home and transferred by the child to the school. This can be applied to bullying. Attachment relationships among children involved in bullying have also been considered, with bullies forming avoidant attachments with carers, while victims may have formed anxious attachments. This research emphasizes the need to understand the development of aggressive behaviour in order to fully understand bullying, as there are clear similarities between the descriptions of the child rearing practices associated with children who behave aggressively and children who engage in bullying.

Brendan Byrne (1993) also discusses some of the familial factors associated with involvement in bullying, and argues that first-born children are more likely to be bullied, possibly because of overprotective child-rearing practices, while bullies are more likely to have aggressive or dominant parents.

Summary

➤ Research has identified a wide range of roles in bullying, including bullies, victims, bully/victims, reinforcer of the bully, defender of the victim and witness.

➤ A number of characteristics have been identified as common among bullies and victims, and these include poor school performance and lower than average popularity.

➤ As with aggression, family factors such as discipline and certain patterns of family relationships have been associated with bullying.

➤ It is important to stress that children involved in bullying may not show any signs of involvement, nor will they definitely reflect the characteristics outlined above.

Tackling bullying

We have already emphasized that although bullying can happen wherever children come together in groups, most research has been done in schools. For similar reasons most of the research on anti-bullying interventions has been done in school settings. Although a wide range of interventions has been described and discussed in the literature, they can be classified under three main headings. Firstly, educational approaches focus on teaching groups of children about the nature of bullying and its effects and giving them the information that will help them to understand how to assess situations where bullying may be occurring. Secondly, participant approaches focus on the individuals and groups that are actively involved in bullying. Finally, environmental approaches involve the alteration of environmental factors that may increase or decrease the likelihood of bullying occurring in a given location.

Interventions can also be classified from the perspective of the groups involved, for example interventions may focus on a single classroom or youth club. In contrast a whole-school intervention involves the staff, pupils and parents in an effort to tackle bullying. Recently, researchers have considered involving the wider community in tackling bullying. However, even on these different levels, interventions will include aspects of the educational, the participant and the environmental approach.

In designing an intervention for a school or a group, it is useful to use a decision-making process that will allow you to identify the areas of action and the methods required. Figure A (p. 30) outlines this process. The first question in this process refers to you and your role within the group. As a practitioner you will probably be faced with serious cases of bullying where you have been asked to work with the victim or the bully. However, you may also be asked to advise other groups in deciding the most appropriate way in which to tackling the problem.

Figure A also includes school principals and teachers; however, these roles are similar to those of the coordinator of a youth club or sports club, and to the youth workers who interact directly with the group or club members. For those in a management role the key action will be around the development and maintenance of policies to prevent bullying and the procedures for dealing with incidences. In addition, principals and coordinators may be involved in dealing with incidents that have been brought to the attention of those working directly with the children, but are more serious or have not been resolved. Finally, as a parent you may want to educate your child about bullying, or be faced with dealing with an incident where your child is the victim or the bully. The next four sections provide information on what can be done by the four groups in more detail.

Section A: Practitioners

By practitioners we refer to professions such as psychologists, counsellors, etc. As an educational psychologist or a counsellor you are more likely to be dealing with serious cases of bullying. There are a number of intervention strategies used to work with victims and bullies individually and within a group setting, particularly by providing children and young people with the skills necessary to respond in a difficult situation. In addition to these, the

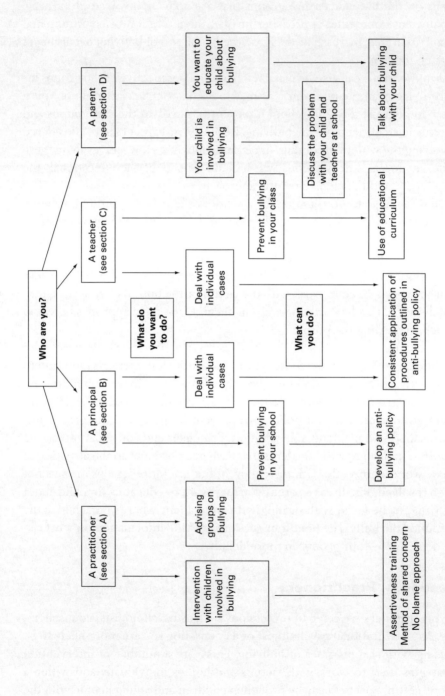

Figure A Tackling bullying: A decision-making process

methods of parent management training and problem-solving skills training outlined in the previous section on aggression can also be used with children involved in bullying.

When asked to work with a child who has been involved in bullying one of the first steps is to identify his or her role. A child can be involved in many ways, such as reinforcing the bully's actions or as a provocative victim, and these may be more difficult to identify. Gather as much information as you can from the child, from his or her parents, and from the school or youth club personnel where the incidents have been occurring. Once you have identified their role you can decide on the most appropriate intervention.

Working with victims of bullying

Victims of bullying may need counselling depending on the extent of the problem. One other method that has been successfully used with victims is assertiveness training. Assertiveness training for victims is outlined by Sharp and Smith (1994, chapter 5) and involves teaching children effective ways of responding to bullying.

Sharp *et al.* (1994) report that this type of intervention is suitable for both primary and secondary schools, with children as young as seven years old. The aim of assertiveness training is to teach children how to respond to a bullying situation, how to get support from witnesses, how to increase their self-esteem and how to extricate themselves from a bullying situation. Sharp *et al.* (1994) provide information on how to structure and carry out an assertiveness course for children. Sharp and Cowie (1994) report that assertiveness training has been found to increase self-esteem, and that a number of studies have shown that bullying decreases following such training.

However, you may have identified the child as a provocative victim, which is one whose actions or behaviours may play a role in their involvement. In this situation you can help the child to identify the situations or actions that may precede an incident which will help them to choose appropriate actions, in addition to developing their self-esteem.

Working with bullies

The 'No Blame' approach (also referred to as the Support Group approach), developed by Barbara Maines and George Robinson (1992), is a method of tackling bullying where a group of bullies is involved in bullying a child or group of children. The group's behaviour is seen as a problem that must be solved and the group (of bullies) is given the responsibility for solving it: no blame for the behaviour is attributed. Often the victim is interviewed to gain insight into the effects of the bullying, but he or she is not included in the problem-solving process. This process works through a series of group discussions with those involved in bullying the victim. During these, the group is presented with the victims' perspective and asked if there are ways they could help. Again, follow-up meetings are used to reinforce positive decisions. Details of Maines and Robinsons's training pack are given in Appendix II.

In evaluating this method, Smith *et al.* (1994) report that case studies have shown positive effects but raise concerns about the way in which cases are selected for discussion. Young (1998) reports on the outcomes of the No Blame Approach in 55 cases where this method was used. She reports that out of 51 cases in primary school, 50 were successfully resolved over time, with 40 showing immediate success.

Working with bullies and victims

The method of 'Common Concern', developed by Pikas (1989), is a method of therapeutically intervening in situations of group bullying. To summarize the process briefly, it involves individual interviews with each of the people involved (bullies and victims), followed by a group meeting with the bullies. These meetings are organized and facilitated by a therapist and focus on developing a shared concern among the group for the victim. Pikas reported that one of the benefits of interviewing the victim was that it assisted the therapist in identifying whether the pupil is a classic or a provocative victim. This allowed the therapist to adjust his or her interactions with the various individuals involved. The end stage of this process was a meeting between the bullies and the victim once the therapist decided that this was appropriate.

Sharp *et al.* (1994) suggest that this method is suitable for use with children from the age of nine years and upward. They outline the three stages involved in the process and also provide scripts for use with both victims and bullies. The three stages are individual meetings of about 10 minutes with each of the children involved, short follow-up interviews again with each individual, and finally a group meeting, with each stage lasting about one week. However, training and practice are essential before this method can be effectively used.

In evaluating this method, Smith *et al.* (1994) report that their experience has been positive. They trained teachers in this method and the feedback was positive. Duncan (1996) reported the results of a survey of 14 adults trained in the use of this method. This study found that, in the 38 cases where this method had been used, 34 were resolved either very successfully or successfully. However, Duncan reports that, in a small number of cases, there were some negative attitudes on the part of parents: among other things the parents wanted the bullies to be punished.

Advising other groups

Apart from this direct contact with children involved in bullying, you may also be asked to advise other groups on bullying. The aim of the following sections is to provide you with information that may be of use to principals, teachers, youth workers or parents.

Summary

> There are a wide variety of methods available for working with children involved in bullying. However, it is important to keep in mind that these methods require training and practice before they can be used.
> Methods used to reduce aggressive behaviour in children can also be used.
> In selecting the most appropriate method, it is important that you gather as much information about the situation from both adults and children.

Section B: School principals and youth organization coordinators

In management roles such as these you may wish to coordinate the development and implementation of an anti-bullying policy within your school or group. An anti-bullying policy should outline both the group's definition of what constitutes bullying and the steps or methods used to tackle the behaviour. Selecting the most appropriate methods is considered below. You must also think about who will be targeted by the policy. In the case of a school, pupils, parents and staff should be considered. The school could also consider the importance of including people outside the school, such as local doctors, community nurses, etc. A youth group may consider coordinating any efforts with a local school, or with other people in the community such as the local community police officer, local health clinics, etc.

For an anti-bullying policy to be effective, every individual within the group must be committed to its implementation. Motivation is seen as the key to organizing and encouraging involvement in this process. However, staff may not be motivated to tackle bullying if they do not think it is an issue within the school. In this case, a survey of involvement in bullying may improve staff members' knowledge of the extent of the problem and as such their willingness to be involved. Methods for carrying out such a survey are outlined below.

When a policy is being developed, it is also necessary to consult parents. This may involve holding an open meeting for parents to discuss the development of the policy, or including parents and teachers or group leaders on a policy development committee. The inclusion of parents in the running of an anti-bullying intervention increases the likelihood that pupils will receive consistent information. Also, children and young people can be included through group or classroom-based discussions on aspects of the policy.

Once the policy has been drafted and reviewed and finally decided upon, it must be consistently, clearly and continually communicated to all the groups involved. This can involve drafting the policy and sending copies to all members, and conference days can be held to outline the policy to the whole group (including parents). Regular updates and reminders can also help maintain the momentum.

There are a number of steps to follow when developing such a policy:

➤ assess your group's value system;
➤ examine your group's definitions of bullying;
➤ identify the extent of the problem;
➤ clearly outline a procedure to follow; and
➤ evaluate with all groups and adapt if necessary.

Assessing the group's value system

All groups have a value system that reflects what is acceptable within the group. Often the school or group's code of conduct will act as the concrete representation of these desired values. This might include how group members should treat other people, both within the group and when representing the group, such as on a school trip. The value system is key in tackling bullying as, by representing what is and is not acceptable behaviour, it should provide a rationale for preventing and tackling bullying.

The starting point is to examine the group's beliefs about the way in which its members are treated and act. When discussing the group's value system there are a number of key considerations. Consider the range of ages within the group and bear in mind the ability of children of all ages to talk about these values. Ask adults to consider the behaviours they encourage and discourage consistently within the group. These can be discussed at a group meeting. Ask young children about what they think are nice ways to treat people and nasty ways to treat them. With older groups it may be useful to discuss what the members of the group see as appropriate and inappropriate. It can also be useful to discuss *why* the group values certain beliefs or behaviours, and why it is important to treat others well, rather than telling the group what is and is not accepted. This can help the group to accept the desired values more readily than if they felt rules are being imposed upon them.

Another important point regarding the group's value system is that the group should not just focus on negative behaviours and what not to do, but also to examine positive behaviours. Following on from this it may be beneficial to develop a system which rewards good behaviour, as well as punishing bad behaviour. However, it should be stressed that as the efforts to tackle bullying continue, the group should become more aware of attitudes towards other negative behaviours.

Once you have identified and clarified the group's central values, it may be useful to simplify the wording used to express them to ensure that they can be understood and remembered by everyone. For example appropriate behaviour and actions could be expressed with the following three rules:

➤ respect yourself;
➤ respect others; and
➤ respect the group's property.

This would be easier for the group to remember and adopt. Once the values are stated clearly and have been communicated to all concerned, discuss with the groups how they could best follow these rules. Perhaps build a group discussion around presenting the group with scenarios and asking them whether the actions of people in the scenarios agree with the values; for example 'If John is angry and kicks the ball at the window, is he respecting the group's property?'

Understanding the group's definition of bullying

In order to tackle bullying, group members must agree on what they are trying to tackle. We have suggested that research and child-focused definitions of bullying appear to differ in several key areas. Exploring the definitions held by the adults and young people involved, be they teachers, group leaders, pupils, club members or parents, can pinpoint any differences between the groups and will allow for the formulation of a definition that is appropriate to that group. This can prevent the members of the group from working at cross-purposes to tackle what could be, in effect, different things.

This process can be carried out using discussion groups, or short interviews around the question, 'what is bullying?' Also, the group could use existing definitions as a guide and look at issues around the behaviours involved, the importance of repetition and intention, the role of power and provocation, etc. Another method that may be more useful for examining younger children's views on bullying is asking them to draw pictures of bullying situations and to discuss some of the aspects of those drawings with the class.

Either method will provide the group with a list of behaviours that are described as bullying, as well as situations where they would or would not be classified as such (e.g. if the victim is upset by the behaviour, it is bullying). While these lists may be long and detailed, identifying the most commonly mentioned behaviours and situations, and including these in the definition of bullying, is a very important step in tackling the problem.

Examining the extent of bullying within the group

In designing an anti-bullying programme there are benefits to assessing the extent and nature of bullying within the school first. An intervention may be more effective when tailored *specifically* to an individual setting. Identifying the extent and nature of the problem within a group can tell you what type of bullying is commonly used, where it takes place, whether children report to adults.

Bullying surveys: There are a number of questionnaires available for identifying the level of involvement in bullying within a group. One of the most common is the 'Bully/victim questionnaire' (Olweus, 1989). This is an anonymous questionnaire completed by pupils and consists of multiple-choice questions about the nature and extent of bullying as they have experienced it. Another is the 'Life in Schools' booklet (Arora and Thompson, 1987), which also looks at reported levels of bullying in the last week but requires pupils to write their name on the form. For further information on surveys Dr Ken Rigby's website (see Appendix II) provides some useful information on bullying questionnaires.

If you are designing a survey yourself there are a number of important sections and questions to include.

➤ Instruct group members not to put their name on the survey and to be as honest as possible in their answers.
➤ Give a definition of bullying. This should reflect the group's definition.
➤ Include a section for children who have been bullied, children who have bullied others and children who may have seen bullying taking place. Each section should begin with the definition and a direct question asking if they have been bullied, bullied others or witnessed bullying. If they answer no to one of these questions they can then move to the next section.
➤ Key questions include what type of bullying was involved (e.g. name-calling, physical harm, exclusion etc), how often the child is involved (e.g. once/twice, several times, once a week etc), where the bullying took place, and whether they have reported the bullying to an adult (for victims and witnesses).
➤ It is important to ask questions in relation to a specific period (e.g. 'Since you came to school in September', 'Since you came back after Christmas' etc). If it is too broad (e.g. 'Have you ever been bullied?') or too

narrow (e.g. 'Have you been bullied this week?') the answers may make it difficult to accurately measure the extent of the problem.

Peer and teacher nominations: Another common method used when identifying bullies and victims is peer or teacher nominations. Here children or teachers are asked to nominate those in the class whom they would classify as either bullies or victims. Peer nominations have been shown to reflect self-reports more so than teacher nominations.

Selecting methods for tackling bullying

In outlining the methods the group will use to tackle bullying, the policy must include both those methods that will be implemented across the school or group (such as an educational curriculum; see section C) and the procedures for dealing with reports of bullying.

Whole group methods: In the wider context of the whole school or group, peer support has been used as a method of tackling bullying. Peer support involves training young people in basic counselling skills and problem-solving techniques so that they can act as a support for children involved in bullying. For readers interested in this method, see Cowie and Wallace (2000) 'Peer Support in Action – From bystanding to standing by'. A major advantage is that these methods provide pupils with the skills to deal with the problem, recognizing the reality that, as an amount of bullying will remain hidden, pupils must be equipped to deal with it.

The group could also consider its general environment and the role it plays in bullying. The idea here is that by altering the environment in which children and young people come together and interact, we can reduce the likelihood that bullying will take place. A bullying survey may have identified the areas where bullying takes place. In the past these have included corridors and stairwells. These areas can be targeted specifically, and adult monitoring increased or access controlled.

One of the main areas for consideration in school is the schoolyard or play area because this is where much of the bullying is likely to take place. Play areas should be stimulating, thus encouraging children to play rather than engage in antisocial activities. Also, providing spaces that encourage all children to actively participate in playground activities can reduce bullying. For example, if only games such as football and basketball are possible, certain pupils will be consistently excluded from the activities.

Procedures for dealing with reports of bullying: Most schools have a procedure in place that outlines how reports of bullying are dealt with. This generally indicates at what point the school principal is involved, at what point parents are called into the school and also what sanctions may be used. One of the key factors in these procedures is that they must be used consistently.

While most schools would use sanctions to deal with bullies, they may not have identified methods for supporting victims. At this point we would suggest working with other professionals, such as educational psychologists, in selecting the methods for dealing with individual victims and bullies, particularly as the methods outlined in section A above require specific training if they are to be used effectively.

Evaluating the effectiveness of the intervention

Once a group has introduced an intervention it is important to evaluate its effectiveness and also consider any necessary changes. One key way of evaluating the effectiveness of the programme is to carry out surveys of involvement in bullying before the policy is introduced and then again after a certain period of time has lapsed. Earlier we outlined some of the questions that can be asked when attempting to survey involvement in bullying. Also, additional questions such as how much change group members think there has been and what aspects were effective can be included.

It may also be useful for the group to discuss how they see the intervention working and to discuss any changes that may be necessary. These discussions should involve representatives of all members of the group, such as parents, pupils and staff in a school setting. Also the school could send a survey home to parents examining their awareness of the programme in the school. Each of the methods outlined in this section should also offer group members the chance to make suggestions on updating and developing the programme. However, it is important to note that the process of evaluation and updating must continue as long as the policy or the intervention is in place.

Summary

➢ In a management capacity it is important to create an environment where positive behaviours are valued and negative behaviours, including bullying, are unacceptable.
➢ An anti-bullying policy which clearly outlines the way in which bullying is dealt with within the group should be developed with input from all parties involved and communicated to the group.
➢ This policy should be consistently implemented and regularly evaluated and updated.

Section C: Teachers/youth club workers

Working with the whole group

Working regularly with your class or group can be one of the most effective ways of both preventing bullying and creating an environment where children are aware that bullying is not acceptable. One of the best ways of working with a group is the development and use of an anti-bullying curriculum: the main aim of an anti-bullying curriculum is to educate the group about the nature of bullying, its effects and how to deal with it. A number of methods and resources are available for use as part of a classroom curriculum, including classroom discussions, drama, videos, role-playing and literature. Appendix II provides information on some of the resources available.

The educational approach can be used in a number of different ways, depending on who is to be educated. A classroom intervention focuses on the pupils within a classroom and may be implemented by the class teacher. This can include discussions around the nature of bullying, discussing the effects of bullying and perhaps agreeing on class rules for dealing with bullying. On a wider level, a school-based intervention may involve educating the staff in the school, as well as the pupils. In addition, a school-based intervention will generally include the parents. The community approach tackles bullying by educating those both within the school and in the wider community about bullying.

Tackling bullying within the wider community is based on the idea that the interactions that lead to bullying may not originate within the school and, indeed, do not necessarily stop at the school gate when pupils are leaving at the end of the day. Byrne (1997) outlined the different levels at which the community approach works, including youth groups and organizations, local police, shop staff, as well as teaching and non-teaching staff within the schools.

There are many benefits to using the educational approach.

➤ It allows adults to tackle existing bullying problems and also to prevent the development of further bullying within the group.
➤ An educational curriculum can be included as part of a school's day-to-day curriculum, which may result in a long-running intervention, rather than one of limited duration.
➤ The implementation of an educational intervention may require less financial investment than other interventions, which may make it very attractive in situations where there are limited financial resources.
➤ There is less need for specialized training for those involved in the implementation of these methods.

One potential limitation of educational approaches is the risk of inconsistency in the messages that children receive about bullying. Firstly, if the programme is being delivered by a number of people both inside and outside the school or group it will require consistent communication of any decisions made or methods used to all those groups, and consistent management of those methods. For example, if teachers are working to encourage children to report all incidents of bullying their work may serve little purpose if the majority of parents discourage children on the grounds that they are 'telling tales'. Also such an intervention, if it is to be included as part of the wider school curriculum, will have to be evaluated and updated on a regular basis in order to ensure its effectiveness.

Working with bullies and victims

One of the first challenges in this situation is identifying bullies and victims. Research has shown that a large number of children who are involved in bullying do not tell teachers or parents. It may be appropriate for teachers or group leaders to talk regularly to children about bullying, and encourage them to tell them if they are having problems. Such communication also ensures that children who are bullying are constantly reminded that their behaviour is unacceptable.

When dealing directly with individual bullies and victims, Olweus (1993) suggested serious talks with both the victim and the bully, which may subsequently involve meeting with their respective parents. However, while this may prevent the bully from continuing his or her behaviour, it does not address the need to support the victim, aside from the benefit of seeing the bully dealt with by teachers or group leaders. The most commonly used approach to bullying in school is to discipline the bullies. This may involve the withdrawal of privileges or detentions. However, it may be more useful for a teacher to consider and discuss why the children are involved in this behaviour.

There are a number of important things to keep in mind in approaching a report of bullying. Firstly, all reports should be considered. At the outset it is important to talk to all those involved and identify exactly what happened. If you feel there is a more serious problem underlying a reported incident, or if this is not the first incident with this group, it can be helpful to invite parents into the school to discuss the situation.

Speaking to parents about bullying can be difficult if the parents of the victim want to protect their child from harm and the parents of the bully feel the need to defend their child's behaviour. It may be more useful to discuss the situation as a problem that must be solved and ask parents for ideas to improve the relations between the children, rather than apportioning blame.

However, in the case of more serious and regular incidents, it may be necessary to involve professionals from outside the school. This should be discussed with the principal and the parents of the children involved. Again, looking at these options as ways of helping the children involved may be a more effective way of ensuring support from the parents.

Summary

➢ It is important to talk openly about bullying and to encourage children to report incidents to an adult.
➢ Be consistent in your dealings with children involved in bullying and follow the guidelines laid down by the school or group.
➢ Children and adults differ in their definitions of bullying; as a result always gather as much information as you can about an alleged incident of bullying.

Section D: Information for parents

As a parent you may be faced with the situation where your child is a bully or a victim. One important issue to keep in mind is the fact that research suggests that adults and children do not necessarily define bullying in the same way. The main implication of this is that while an adult may feel that a child was bullying, the child may not perceive his or her actions in the same way. As such any discussion of bullying with a child should examine their perception or understanding of the behaviour in general or a specific incident.

Educating your child about bullying

The key to tackling bullying is consistency. With this in mind, a good starting point for discussing bullying with your child is to speak to the school about any existing guidelines or any policy statements they may have. It is also essential to encourage your child to talk about bullying and to discuss their ideas about what bullying is. It is important to reassure your child that if they are involved in bullying, they can talk to you about it. By encouraging your child to discuss bullying in general they should feel more comfortable discussing their own experiences with you.

One useful method for discussing bullying with your child is to use books and stories that refer to bullying situations. By using these books, you can ask you child about the characters' behaviours and discuss their responses with them, perhaps looking at the best way to act in the various situations. Also, children's television programmes sometimes deal with bullying and this can be a good opportunity to discuss the behaviour with your child.

Another key to preventing your child's involvement is to be consistent in how you respond to their behaviour at home. Encourage them to treat others fairly and clarify when their behaviour is unacceptable. Earlier in this booklet (pp. 19–20), we outlined methods for encouraging positive behaviour and discouraging negative behaviour in relation to aggression. These methods can be applied to aspects of bullying behaviour, too; however, the key is consistency.

If your child is involved in bullying

Identifying whether your child is involved in bullying (either as a bully or as a victim) can be very difficult. Unfortunately, research suggests that we cannot always rely on children telling adults about bullying incidents. As a result, you should be aware that bullying might be taking place even when incidents are not being reported.

A number of books have suggested signs to watch out for if you think a child is involved in bullying. These may include a child being frightened or unwilling to go to school, or returning home with unexplained bruises or damaged belongings. However, many children who are being bullied may not show any of these signs. It should be stressed that these symptoms will, at best, only identify the victims of bullying and give no indication that a child is bullying another. The best way to ensure that you are aware of your child's involvement in bullying activity is to encourage him or her to talk about their experiences and to tell someone if they have worries or concerns.

If your child tells you that they are being bullied, a good starting point is to discuss the incidents with your child and gather as much information as possible. Also, it is important to ask your child how they would like you to help them. Children can feel that the handling of the situation is taken out of their hands and that their views on how they would like the problem dealt with are ignored.

It can be difficult for parents to accept that their child is involved in bullying others. If you discover that your child is involved, again we would suggest discussing the situation with your child and gathering as much information as you can. It is useful to view the situation as a problem that must be tackled by all the parties involved, both children and adults, where the solution is to the benefit of all involved. Helping your child to change their involvement can prevent problems later in life. Finally, some of the methods discussed in the previous section for dealing with aggressive children can also be applied to bullying.

Summary

➤ While it can be difficult to discover that your child is being bullied or bullying others, keep in mind that a child can be involved in bullying while both teachers and parents remain unaware.

➤ Discuss bullying openly with your child, perhaps using books or stories that raise the issue.

➤ Be consistent in your responses to your child's negative behaviour.

Involving children in tackling bullying

In recent times, researchers have begun to consider how children can be involved in tackling bullying. As bullying takes place away from adults but in the presence of peers, the peer group should be included in any intervention aimed at reducing levels of bullying. Also, it has been argued that the involvement of pupils may add to the effectiveness of an intervention. Although some interventions have included group discussions of bullying, this has generally been as part of an intervention rather than a way in which children can be involved in the development of an intervention. A number of studies have shown that children are capable of offering solutions to bullying, and as such it is important to involve them.

There are many ways in which children can be involved in anti-bullying interventions, and one of the most common has been through the use of quality circles. During this process, children devise solutions to bullying scenarios and these are then presented to the school. For a detailed description of using quality circles in a school setting see Cowie and Sharp (1994).

Summary

➤ Involving children in tackling bullying is seen as central to the success of any intervention.

➤ Children have been shown to be capable of providing useful input into school-based interventions, as well as alternative solutions to bullying.

Conclusions

Children's aggression can be a cause of great concern to parents. No one likes to see children causing physical or mental distress to one another. Unfortunately most children will show some undesirable aggressive behaviour on occasions and parents need to make it clear that such behaviour is unacceptable, as well as commenting favourably when children find nonaggressive ways to resolve their differences. For some children aggression will become a problem. These children may continue to show high levels of physical aggression as they move from their preschool years into the early years of primary school at a time when their peers have stopped being physically aggressive. Unfortunately these children may be rejected by their peer group, which can compound their problems.

Although it is not possible to say why one child is more aggressive than another, research suggests that certain family and personal factors may increase the risk of aggression. These factors include a lack of warmth in the parent–child relationships, parents' use of power assertive disciplinary practices and problems with processing some types of social information. Fortunately, research suggests that intervention can help children to overcome these problems, particularly when the intervention takes place early in the child's life.

Children spend a lot of time in the company of their peers at home, in playgrounds and in school. It is inevitable, therefore, that at times aggressive behaviour can become part of the pattern of interaction between children in these settings. The term bullying has been used to describe this social form of aggression. Bullying can take the form of direct verbal or physical attacks on children or it may take the form of intimidation, threats or excluding some children from group activities. Research suggests that bullying is widespread in schools in Britain and Ireland, where it may be experienced by up to one-third of children. Despite the fact that bullying has short- and long-term negative consequences for children and that it can make many children extremely unhappy, the research suggests that such behaviour is typically not reported to adults in authority. Unfortunately this means that many adults who work with groups of children may be unaware of the extent to which bullying is a problem within the group.

Although the majority of children who bully others only do so occasionally, there is a group of children who bully regularly, and research suggests that the family backgrounds of these children are very similar to the family backgrounds of children who have problems with aggressive behaviour. Interventions to tackle bullying may focus on raising awareness of the problem in the school or community, therapeutic work with bullies and victims or changing in the school environment in constructive ways. Whatever approach to intervention is chosen, it should involve the children themselves in order to ensure that their perspective on bullying is understood and to encourage their sense of involvement in the intervention.

References

Arora, C. M. J., & Thompson, D. A. (1987). Defining bullying for a secondary school. *Education and Child Psychology*, *4*, 110–120.

Bates, J. E., & Bayles, K. (1988). Attachment and the development of behavior problems. In J. Belsky & T. Nezworski (eds), *Clinical Implications of Attachment*, Hillsdale, NJ: Erlbaum. pp. 253–99.

Byrne, B. (1993). *Coping with Bullying in Schools*. Dublin: Columba Press.

Byrne, B. (1997). Bullying: A community approach. *Irish Journal of Psychology*, *18(2)*, 258–66.

Coie, J. D., & Dodge, K. A. (1998). Aggression and antisocial behavior. In W. Damon (series ed.) & N. Eisenberg (vol. ed) *Handbook of Child Psychology: Vol. 3. Social, Emotional and Personality Development*, New York: Wiley.

Coie, J. D., Terry, R., Lenox, K., Lochman, J. E., & Hyman, C. (1995). Childhood peer rejection, aggression as predictors of stable patterns of adolescent disorder. *Development and Psychopathology*, *7*, 697–713.

Cowie, H., & Sharp, S. (1994). How to tackle bullying through the curriculum. In S. Sharp & P.K. Smith, (eds), *Tackling Bullying in Your School: A Practical Handbook for Teachers*. London: Routledge.

Cowie, H. & Wallace, P., (2000). *Peer Support in Action – From Bystanding to Standing By*. London, Sage.

Dodge, K. A. (1985). A social information processing model of social competence in children. In M. Perlmutter (ed.), *Cognitive Perspectives on Children's Social and Behavioral Development: Minnesota Symposium on Child Psychology (Vol. 18)*. Hillsdale, NJ: Erlbaum.

Duncan, A. (1996). The shared concern method for resolving group bullying in schools. *Educational Psychology in Practice*, *12(2)*, 94–8.

Dunn, J. (1993). From preschool to adolescence: A ten-year follow-up of siblings in Cambridge. Presented to Centre for Family Research Cambridge. Cited in Loeber, R., & Hay, D. (1997). Key issues in the development of aggression and violence from childhood to early adulthood, *Annual Review of Psychology*, *48*, 371–410.

Farrington, D. P. (1993). Understanding and preventing bullying. In M. Tonry & N. Morris (eds.), *Crime and Justice: An Annual Review of Research*, *Vol. 17*. Chicago: University of Chicago Press.

Farrington, D. P., & Hawkins, J. D. (1991). Predicting participation, early onset and later persistence in officially recorded offending. *Criminal Behavior and Mental Health*, *1*, 1–33.

Huesmann, L. R., Eron, L. D., Lefkowitz, M. M., & Walder, L. O. (1984). Stability of aggression over time and generations. *Developmental Psychology*, *20*, 1120–34.

Kazdin, A. E. (1987). Treatment of antisocial behavior in children: Current status and future directions. *Psychological Bulletin*, *102*, 187–203.

Kazdin, A. E. (1993). Treatment of conduct disorder: Progress and directions in psychotherapy research. *Development and Psychopathology*, *5*, 277–310.

Loeber, R., & Hay, D. (1997). Key issues in the development of aggression and violence from childhood to early adulthood, *Annual Review of Psychology*, *48*, 371–410.

Maines, B., & Robinson, G. (1992). *The No Blame Approach*. Bristol: Lucky Duck.

O'Moore, A. M., Kirkham, C. & Smith, M. (1997). Bullying behaviour in Irish schools: A nationwide study. *Irish Journal of Psychology*, *18(2)*, 141–69.

Olweus, D. (1979). Stability and aggressive reaction patterns in males: A review. *Psychological Bulletin*, *86*, 852–75.

Olweus, D. (1989). *Bully/victim questionnaire*. Unpublished questionnaire. University of Bergin, Norway.

Olweus, D. (1993). *Bullying: What We Know and What We Can Do*. Oxford: Blackwell Publishers.

Patterson, G. R., & Bank, C. L. (1989). Some amplifying mechanisms for pathological processes in families. In M. Gunnar & E. Thelen (eds.), *Systems and Development: Symposia on Child Psychology*. Hillsdale, NJ: Erlbaum.

Pikas, A. (1989). The common concern method for the treatment of mobbing. In E. Roland & E. Munthe (eds.), *Bullying: An International Perspective*. London: David Fulton Publishers.

Sharp. S. & Cowie, H. (1994). Empowering pupils to take positive action against bullying. In P. K. Smith & S. Sharp (eds.), *School Bullying: Insights and Perspectives*. London: Routledge.

Sharp, S., Cowie, H., & Smith, P. K. (1994). How to respond to bullying behaviour. In S. Sharp & P. K. Smith (eds.), *Tackling Bullying in Your School: A Practical Handbook for Teachers*. London: Routledge.

Sharp, S. & Smith, P. K. (eds) (1994). *Tackling Bullying in Your School: A Practical Handbook for Teachers*. London: Routledge.

Smith, P. K. (1991). Bullying: The silent nightmare. *The Psychologist, 4*, 243–8.

Smith, P. K., Cowie, H., & Sharp, S. (1994). Working directly with pupils involved in bullying situations. In P. K. Smith & S. Sharp (eds.), *School Bullying: Insights and Perspectives*. London: Routledge.

Smith, P. K. & Sharp, S. (1994). The problem of school bullying. In P. K. Smith & S. Sharp (eds.), *School Bullying: Insights and Perspectives*. London: Routledge.

Whitney, I., & Smith, P. K. (1993). A survey of the nature and extent of bullying in junior/middle and secondary schools. *Education Research, 35*, 3–25.

Young, S. (1998). The support group approach to bullying in school. *Educational Psychology in Practice, 14(1)*, 32–9.

Appendix I: Assessing aggression

1. Definition

The first step in assessing a child's behaviour is to come up with a list of the behaviours that you will define as aggression. Because aggression takes many forms a complete list would be extremely long; however, the list below contains three of the main types of aggressive behaviour and the behaviours so classified.

Physical aggression:

- hits
- punches
- kicks
- jostles
- pulls hair
- pinches

Verbal aggression:

- name-calls
- shouts
- uses abusive language

Indirect aggression:

- excludes from group
- says nasty things about others

It is most important that everyone involved in the intervention with an individual child agrees on what constitutes aggressive behaviour so the final list should be agreed among parents, teachers, therapists and everyone else involved with the child.

2. Observing and recording

Although a parent or teacher may be very certain that a child's aggressive behaviour is sufficiently frequent for it to be a cause for concern, it is still important to find a way to measure that behaviour. Measuring the behaviour provides you with a baseline indication of the extent of the problem and allows you to assess the effectiveness of any intervention by examining how much the behaviour has changed. If you include a timeframe in your recording you may also get further clues to the factors contributing to the behaviour. For example, if tiredness is a contributory factor, then you would expect to see aggression increasing in the evening in the hours before bedtime. Below is a sample timesheet that could be used to measure aggressive behaviour over one day. The day has been divided into two-hour sections, and there is space for tallies corresponding to each of the three types of aggression described above.

Aggression Recording Sheet

Name: Date:

Key: PA = Physical aggression, e.g. hits, punches, kicks; VA = Verbal aggression, e.g. calls names, uses abusive language; IA = Indirect aggression, e.g. excludes child from group

---

8.00–10.00 PA

VA

IA

10.00–12.00 PA

VA

IA

12.00–14.00 PA

VA

IA

14.00–16.00 PA

VA

IA

16.00–18.00 PA

VA

IA

18.00–20.00 PA

VA

IA

20.00–22.00 PA

VA

IA

Appendix II: Bullying resources

There is a wide range of resources available to individuals and groups concerned about bullying. The following is just a selection of some of the books, organizations and websites where information can be gained.

Books

There is a growing range of books and resource packs available for children, parents, teachers, researchers and other professionals. We have suggested some titles below, along with a short description of the book, and some suggestions on who might be interested in reading it.

- ➤ Byrne, B. (1993). *Coping with Bullying in Schools*. Dublin: Columba Press. This is a good book for both teachers and parents on bullying in school. It provides information on research into the background to, and extent of, involvement in bullying, as well as outlining some methods of preventing and tackling bullying.
- ➤ Cowie, H. and Wallace, P. (2000). *Peer Support in Action – From Bystanding to Standing By*. London: Sage. Focusing on one method that has been used to tackle bullying, this book provides the reader with the theoretical background and the practical advice behind developing and using peer support.
- ➤ Elliot, M. (1995). *Teenscape: A Personal Safety Programme for Teenagers*. London: Health Education Authority. This is a guide for teachers, parents and other adults to some of the issues affecting young people, including bullying. Provides some practical methods for tackling bullying, such as classroom-based discussion.
- ➤ Maines, B., and Robinson, G. (1992). *The No Blame Approach*. Bristol: Lucky Duck. This video and booklet pack describes a method for teachers to work with children directly involved in bullying. It is available from Lucky Duck Publishing Ltd., 10 South Terrace, Redlands, Bristol, BS6 6TG, UK.
- ➤ Mellor, A. (1997). *Bullying at School: Advice for Families*. Edinburgh: SCRE.

This book provides information for families on what bullying is, how to deal with the school when your child is involved in bullying, signs to help parents spot if their child is being bullied, as well as further reading on the issue.

➤ Munn, P. (1993). *Supporting Schools against Bullying*. Edinburgh: SCRE. This pack provides information for schools on tackling bullying, involving parents and non-teaching staff within the school, practical activities and methods for identifying the extent of involvement in the school. Could also be used by youth groups, etc.

➤ Olweus, D. (1993). *Bullying:What We Know and What We Can Do*. Oxford: Blackwell Publishers.
Based on research carried out by the author in Scandinavia, this book provides information on the nature and extent of bullying, and the factors associated with it, as well as practical advice on the development and use of a whole school anti-bullying programme. This book provides useful information for teachers and parents, and can be used by youth club leaders, etc.

➤ Sharp, S. and Smith, P. (1994). *Tackling Tackling Bullying in Your School: A Practical Handbook for Teachers*. London: Routledge.
This book provides the reader with a guide to developing strategies to tackle bullying. While it has been written for teachers specifically and looks at methods that can be used in school, much of the information could be adapted for use in youth groups and sports clubs.

➤ Smith, P. K. and Sharp, S. (1994). *School Bullying: Insights and Perspectives*. London: Routledge.
A very useful review of research in the area of bullying interventions, this book provides information on research studies which have examined the extent of involvement in bullying, bullying and special needs, as well as intervention methods such as whole-school policies, educational curriculum, and peer support. This book provides more a theoretical review of the subject than practical suggestion.

Organizations

Anti-bullying Centre	Trinity College Dublin, Dublin 2, Ireland
Anti-bullying Network	Faculty of Education, University of Edinburgh, Holyrood Road, Edinburgh, EH8 8AQ, Scotland http://antibullying.net
Countering Bullying Unit	UWIC, Cyncoed, Cardiff, CF23 6XD, Wales
KIDSCAPE	152 Buckingham Palace Road, London, SW1W 9TR, England http://www.kidscape.org.uk/kidscape

Websites

Using the key words 'bully' or 'bullying' as part of a general web search will provide you with a wide range of bullying information websites. Those listed below are just some of the sites available. However, the authors are not responsible for the content or availability of these sites.

➢ Bullying Online www.bullying.co.uk
  Produced by the Anti-Bullying Campaign group, this site includes advice for teachers, parents and children. Topics covered include policy information, legal advice for parents, information from the Department for Education and Employment as well as practical projects and exercises for schools.
➢ Bullying at school www.scre.ac.uk/bully
  This site is produced by the Scottish Council for Research in Education and provides information on bullying in school, including what families and schools can do, as well as links for further information.
➢ Bullying www.lfcc.on.ca/bully.htm
  This Canadian-based site is produced by the London Family Court Clinic in Ontario and provides information for parents and teachers on bullying research and interventions.
➢ Childline www.ChildLine.org.uk/factsheets/bullying1.htm
  This fact sheet was developed by Childline and provides information for children and adults on issues such as 'What is bullying?', 'Are you a bully?' and where to go for help and information.
➢ Dr Ken Rigby's page www.education.unisa.edu.au/bullying
  This Australian page provides information from research about bullying. It also provides general information on the use of questionnaires to find out about bullying among children and young people.

➤ No Blame Approach www.luckyduck.co.uk
  Lucky Duck publishes resources on a wide range of topics, including bullying. Developed by Barbara Maines and George Robinson, it provides information on a wide range of products for tackling bullying.

➤ No Bully Site www.nobully.org.nz
  This site, based in New Zealand, provides information for parents, carers and teachers on the Stop Bullying Campaign, as well as on resources and contacts. It also provides information for children on what bullying is, and how to get help and advice on bullying.

➤ UK DFES www.dfes.gov.uk/bullying/index.shtml
  This is the UK Department for Education and Skill's bullying page. It provides information on bullying in school for pupils, parents and teachers. It also includes details of the recently revised 'Bullying: Don't suffer in silence' pack published by the Department for Education and Employment (DFEE), as it was then called (2nd edn, 2000).